S0-BIW-925

ANIMAL LIVES

ANIMAL LIVES

Written by

CECILIA FITZSIMONS

Illustrated by

Adam Hook

RSVP

RAINTREE
STECK-VAUGHN
PUBLISHERS
The Steck-Vaughn Company

Austin, Texas

FRANKLIN PIERCE
COLLEGE LIBRARY
RINDGE, N.H. 03461

© **Copyright, this edition, 1996 Steck-Vaughn Company.**

All rights reserved. No part of the material protected by this copyright may be reproduced

or utilized in any form or by any means, electronic or mechanical, including photocopying, recording, or by

any information storage and retrieval system, without permission in

writing from the copyright owner. Requests for permission to make copies of any part of

the work should be mailed to :

Copyright Permissions, Steck-Vaughn Company, P.O. Box 26015, Austin, TX 78755

Published by Raintree Steck-Vaughn, an imprint of Steck-Vaughn Company

Library of Congress Cataloging-in-Publication Data

Fitzsimons, Cecilia

Animal lives / written by Cecilia Fitzsimons; illustrated by Adam Hook.

p.   cm. — (Nature's hidden worlds)

Includes index.

Summary: Text and picture puzzles illustrate how animals behave during their lives.

ISBN 0-8172-3968-5 (Hardcover)

ISBN 0-8172-4182-5 (Softcover)

1. Animal behavior—Juvenile literature. 2. Animals—Juvenile literature.

[1. Animals—Habits and behavior. 2. Animals. 3. Picture puzzles.] I. Hook, Adam, ill. II. Title. III. Series.

QL751.5.F55   1996

591.51—dc20

95-18463

CIP   AC

Note to reader

There are some words in this book that are printed in **bold** type. You will

find the meanings for each of these words in the glossary on page 46.

Puzzle illustrations designed and painted by Adam Hook

Designer: Mike Jolley

Project Editor: Wendy Madgwick

Editor: Kim Merlino

Printed in Italy

1 2 3 4 5 6 7 8 9 LB 99 98 97 96

curr
QL
751.5
.F55
1996

Introduction

To survive, animals have to find food to eat, a place to live, and a mate to produce young. This book shows some of the ways that animals behave during their lives. Each picture involves a puzzle. Which animal built which home? Find the migration routes of the birds. Spot the animal families that do not live in Africa. As you solve the puzzles, you will learn about how animals live and the way they behave.

Contents

On Guard

Life is full of problems for living things. Animals have to compete for food, mates, and a place to live. They do this in many ways. Look at these two pictures of the animals that live on the edge of a European **moor**. Can you spot ten differences between them?

Most animals need three main things in order to live and produce young. They need food to eat, a place to live, and a mate. Sometimes these things are in short supply. An animal may then have to fight in order to get them.

Many animals have their own home area called a **territory**. They protect this home base and its supply of food against other animals. Often they use sounds, colors, or ways of holding their bodies to warn rivals and enemies. Sometimes they fight.

In the breeding season, adult animals need to attract a mate. They also need to warn off their rivals. They do this in many ways.

This Is My Home

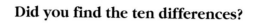

Did you find the ten differences?

1   A red deer stag's antler has another prong.

2   A young male stag has lost his antlers.

3   Another young male stag is present.

4   The hare's ears are drooping.

5   A female red deer's head has moved.

6   A red deer stag's mane is longer.

7   The European robin on the twig is calling.

8   The male pheasant's color is different.

9   A male grouse is displaying its feathers.

10 A female grouse is present.

The male European robin sings a beautiful song. This attracts a female. It also warns other males that "this is my territory." Another male robin may attack the singer. This may lead to a fight. The territory will belong to the winning bird.

Other male birds such as the pheasant display their beautiful feathers. The color of their plumage varies a great deal. The female is almost always a dull brown. One male tries to attract several females. The most colorful males seem to attract the most mates.

Several male grouse compete in a special display area called a lek. The females watch nearby. The males call, dance, and spread their tails to attract the females. A successful male will attract several females to his part of the lek.

In spring, male hares chase each other around a field. They leap in the air and box with their paws to attract a female.

Male red deer, like other male deer, grow a new set of antlers each summer. At the beginning of the rut, or breeding season, each stag gathers his own herd of females. He walks around them, throwing his head back and bellowing. During the rut, stags mark their territory with scent. They grow a long shaggy coat and roll in mud. Fighting stags strike their antlers together but rarely hurt each other. Younger males watch nearby waiting to see which stag will win.

Branching out

Each year in early summer, a stag grows a new set of antlers. At first they are bony knobs covered with a furry skin called velvet. This contains the blood vessels that take blood to the growing antlers. The antlers grow quickly. By the end of summer, they have finished growing. The velvet shrivels and dies. The stag removes it by rubbing his antlers against bushes and trees. Underneath, the antlers are white shiny bone. The deer sheds its antlers between January and April. The antlers get larger and more branched each year.

2 Animal Families

Many animals live in family groups or large herds. Look carefully at this picture of some animal families found in southern Africa. Can you spot the ten animals that do not live in Africa?

For many animals, living in a family group is safer than living alone. Grazing animals face special dangers. They graze on wide open grasslands where they cannot hide from their predators. They are in greatest danger when they are eating the grass. Then their head is held down, near to the ground. They cannot easily see their enemies.

In a **herd**, there are always a few animals keeping watch. If one animal sees danger, it warns the others. Then they can all run away. If the herd is attacked, only one animal may be caught. The rest have a chance to escape.

Wildebeest (A), gemsbok (B), and zebra (C) live in large herds. Some herds contain both males and females. Others are made up of only one sex.

Working Together

Animal families from other parts of the world

1. The rhea from South America looks like an ostrich. The male looks after the chicks.

2. The bison from North America lives in small family herds.

3. The llama comes from South America. Each male has a herd of females.

4. European red deer females and young live in a herd. Stags live in male herds.

5. Przewalski's horse lived in large herds in Europe. It is now **extinct** in the wild.

6. The ring-tailed lemur from Madagascar uses its tail to signal to family members.

7. The Indian tiger, such as this cub, is very rare. Little is known of its family life. It will soon be extinct if poaching continues.

8. The Arctic hare often lives alone. It gathers in large herds on the **tundra** in autumn and winter.

9. The European badger lives with its family in an underground **burrow**.

10. The prairie dog from North America lives in huge underground towns. They call and bark to each other and "kiss" to recognize family members.

Young male wildebeest stay with their mothers for nine months. Then, they join the male herds. Young zebra stay with the herd for about two years. The young males are driven out by the **dominant** male. They will form a herd of their own. Gemsbok have mixed herds of males, females, and young.

Ostriches (D) live in flocks. A male ostrich mates with several females. The male helps care for the eggs and chicks. Often the chicks from more than one female are cared for together. There can be up to forty chicks in a brood.

Some members of animal families have a close relationship with each other. Lions (E) live in a close family group called a pride. The lionesses hunt together and share the kill with the males and cubs. By playing with older animals, the cubs are taught to hunt, fight, and survive.

Meerkat (F) families live underground. During the day they sun themselves. Several meerkats guard the nest watching for danger. Some keep watch from a high point, while others stay on the ground. Some meerkats hunt for food. Others are nurses, guarding the young.

Family against family

In the Far North, a family of musk oxen graze on the short tundra plants. Slowly, carefully, a pack of hungry wolves track the musk oxen. The wolf pack splits to attack from both sides. The adult oxen form a tight circle around their baby calves. Their heads and horns all face outward. The horns make good weapons to ward off the wolves. The wolves circle around but cannot reach the baby calves. Eventually they give up and slink away.

Elephants (G) have one of the most caring family units. A herd is made up of females and young. Males live alone. The herd protects young and sick animals. When an elephant dies, the others stay by the body for many hours before leaving.

3

A Micro World

Army ants eat everything in their path. They leave clear trails behind them. The antbird follows the ants. Look at this picture of a forest floor in South America. Can you find the one clear trail that will lead the antbird (A) to the ant's nest (B)?

The rain forests of South America are home to many kinds of animals. Numerous tiny creatures scurry among the leaves of the forest floor. In this micro world beneath your feet hunters and the hunted live out their lives.

Many kinds of ants live in these forests. Most of them build a permanent **nest**. Army ants do not. They swarm across the forest floor eating everything in their path. When they rest they make a temporary nest called a bivouac. This is made up of a thick mass of ants. Worker and soldier ants link legs and use their bodies to build the nest. The queen ant lives inside with her eggs and **larvae**.

Every morning soldier ants leave the camp and march away in a column to hunt for food. Any animal caught in their path is attacked, stung, and eaten. They cut up their prey with their large sharp jaws. The small worker ants carry the ant-sized pieces of food back to the camp.

Not all kinds of ants hunt. Leaf-cutting ants cut out tiny pieces of leaf. They carry these back to their nest. Worker ants chew the green leaves into a spongy mass.

Mouse opossum

The mouse opossum is a **marsupial**. It is a distant relative of kangaroos and koala bears. Unlike most marsupials, the opossum does not have a pouch. The female carries up to five babies around on her back.

Beneath Your Feet

Other worker ants take this leaf compost to garden chambers where a fungus grows. The fungus is the main food of the ant colony.

Antbirds search the undergrowth for insects to eat. They often follow the columns of army ants. They catch the insects that flee from the path of the soldier ants.

The tiny mouse opossum is smaller than some of the insects it eats. The mouse opossum climbs well. In the day, it rests in tree holes or old birds' nests.

The huge Hercules beetle, up to 6 inches (15 cm) long, eats mainly fruit. The males have long horns. They use them to fight each other.

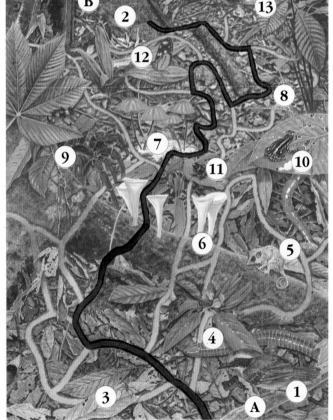

Whom did you pass on the trail?

1 Antbird looking for insects.
2 Army ants in their bivouac.
3 Leaf-cutting ants collecting pieces of leaf.
4 Caecilian, a type of amphibian.
5 Mouse opossum.
6 Cup fungi.
7 Parasol fungi.
8 Giant centipede.
9 Bird-eating spider.
10 Yellow poison arrow frog.
11 Red poison arrow frog.
12 Postman (Ithiomid) butterfly.
13 Hercules beetle.

Many rain forest animals are poisonous. For example, tropical centipedes are fierce hunters. Some grow to 12 inches (30 cm) long. A centipede's front legs form poison claws. It attacks its prey with these claws and injects a poison. Large bird-eating spiders also inject their prey with poison. They eat insects and small birds and mammals. The skin of poison arrow frogs contains a very strong poison. Their bright colors warn predators to leave these frogs alone.

Many insects, such as the postman butterfly, are also brightly colored. The colorful caecilian is an amphibian, related to frogs. These blind, burrowing animals can grow to 4 feet (over 1 m) in length.

Rain forests have a wealth of plant life. Fungi and bacteria help rot down plant and animal remains on the forest floor. Tiny parasol fungi and cup fungi grow there. Like many plants, they are used by local people to make medicines. Some have proved very important.

Ant families

Ants are social insects. This means they live and work together in a **colony**. The queen ant is huge and is the only ant to lay eggs. She lives in the center of the nest and is tended by thousands of worker ants. Some workers are larger than the others. They have large heads and jaws. These are the soldier ants. They hunt and protect the colony. The queen lays her eggs almost continually. The eggs hatch into larvae. They will develop into more workers.

At certain times of the year, some larvae develop into winged females and males. When they are adults, these ants swarm and fly away from the old nest. They mate, then shed their wings. They start to make a new nest. The female will become the new queen and form a new colony.

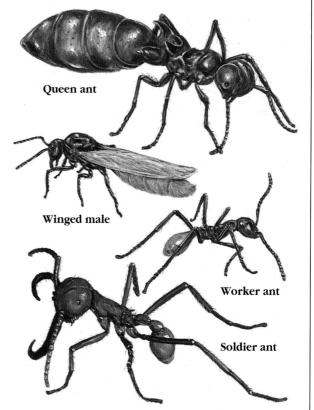

Queen ant

Winged male

Worker ant

Soldier ant

Changing Shape

The young of many insects and amphibians are totally unlike their parents. Look carefully at this picture of a pond. Can you match the six adults in the small pictures with their young? Now look at the picture again. Can you find four more insects and their larvae?

The **life cycle** of insects and amphibians (frogs, toads, and salamanders) has several different stages. The young often look very different from the adults.

The common frog and the palmate newt, a salamander, are amphibians. They spend most of their adult life on land. Then, they return to water to breed and lay their eggs. The eggs hatch into larvae that will live in the water. The larvae feed and grow. Slowly they grow legs, and their bodies change shape. They turn into tiny adults. Frog tadpoles have round bodies. Newt larvae have long bodies with feathery gills.

The Cycle of Life

The adults and their young

1. Palmate newt and larva.
2. Cabbage white butterfly and caterpillars (larvae).
3. Great diving beetle and larva.
4. Emperor dragonfly and nymph.
5. Common frog and tadpole.
6. Stag beetle and grub (larva).
7. Mayfly and larva.
8. Caddis fly and larva.
9. Drone fly and rat-tailed maggot (larva).
10. Chironomid midge and bloodworm (larva).

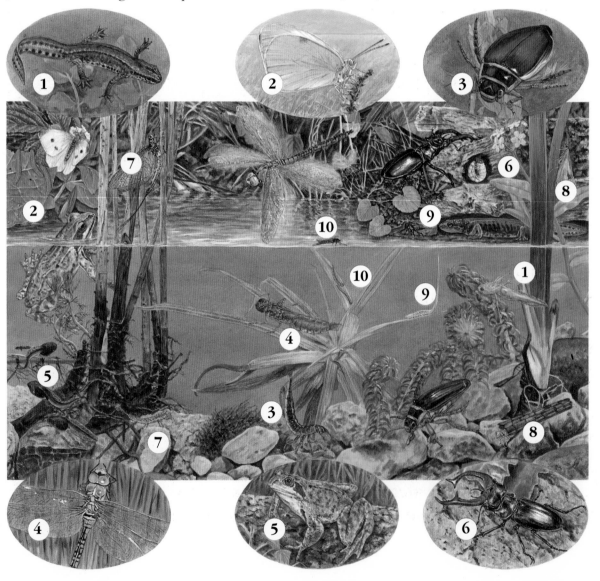

Insects also have several stages in their life cycle. After mating, a female cabbage white butterfly lays her eggs on a leaf. She chooses plants from the cabbage family. The eggs hatch into caterpillars that eat the leaf. These tiny caterpillars grow very quickly.

After several weeks, the caterpillar changes into a **pupa**. Inside the pupa, the caterpillar's body is broken down and built up again. During this stage, the insect changes into a butterfly. The pupa splits open and the adult butterfly crawls free. The butterfly spreads its wings to let them dry in the sun. Then it flies away to mate and lay its eggs.

Stag beetles have a similar life cycle. The eggs are laid in decaying wood. They hatch into larvae called grubs. The grubs feed on the rotting wood. Then they burrow into the wood and change into pupae. The following spring the adult stag beetle crawls out.

Other insects lay their eggs in the pond. Adult dragonflies hunt other flying insects. The females lay their eggs in water. The nymph that hatches hunts other water animals. Adult diving beetles live in water.

A slow change

Butterflies and beetles have four stages in their life cycle. The egg hatches into a larva. The larva becomes a pupa and the pupa hatches into the adult. In other insects the larva, or **nymph**, slowly changes into an adult. There is no pupal stage. The nymph molts, or sheds its skin, as it grows. After each molt the nymph looks more like an adult. This dragonfly nymph is similar to its parent. Can you see the tiny wing buds on its back?

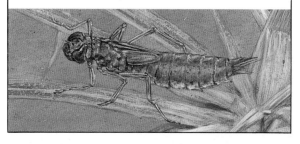

They swim using their powerful limbs. Diving beetles also have wings to fly from one pond to another. Diving beetle larvae are fierce predators. They catch insects and tadpoles and even small fish.

Mayfly larvae have three long tail filaments. The larvae of chironomid midges are called bloodworms because of their bright red color. The drone fly larva is called a rat-tailed maggot. It breathes through its long, tubelike tail. A caddis fly lays its eggs in water. The larva builds a shell-like home from pieces of reed, stones, or other materials.

5

Growing Up

Many young animals depend on their parents for food and a home. Later their parents teach them how to find food and survive on their own. Look carefully at these pictures of a ror in North America. Can you spot the ten differences betwee

Birds and mammals take greater care of their young than any other type of animal. Chicks and babies are raised in a safe, warm nest. They are fed and kept clean. Later, the parents teach their young the skills they need to survive on their own.

Grizzlies eat a variety of foods. These include plants, roots, berries, and insects, as well as animals as big as a moose. The cubs must learn from their mother which foods they can eat. She also teaches them how to collect or catch the food. Bears come together each year to catch the salmon in mountain rivers. Some bears fight over the best places to fish. Cubs learn to fish, but they also learn how to behave with other bears.

Learning About Life

The female raccoon teaches her young to climb trees and swim. She also shows them how to find food in water and on land. Beaver cubs help their parents. They learn how to use branches to dam rivers and build their lodge.

Feed me!

In addition to learning, animals behave by instinct. This means that they do not have to learn certain actions. They just know how to do them. Their brains already carry the information that they need, just like a computer program. Baby birds instinctively open their beaks and call for food. They only do this when their parents return to the nest. Each chick's mouth is bright yellow or orange inside. This color guides the parents and encourages them to put food into the chick's mouth.

Pileated woodpecker

Puma cubs practice their hunting and fighting skills by playing with each other. They also watch their parents hunt. The cubs will learn which animals are easily caught and which can defend themselves. Skunks defend their young against predators. They spray their enemies with a foul smelling liquid. These wolf cubs will quickly learn not to try to catch a skunk again!

The female deer protects her young in a different way. She raises her white tail like a flag to signal danger. The fawn easily follows her white tail as they run away. Only the males have antlers for protection.

Some animals use sounds to signal to one another and their young. Wolves bark and howl to each other during the hunt. Coyotes howl at night to keep in touch across long distances.

Most birds hatch and raise their chicks in a nest. Birds spend less time teaching their young than do most mammals. The blue jay hides its nest among the branches of a conifer tree. Pileated woodpeckers nest in a hollow tree. Their chicks are fed until they can fly and leave the nest. The young birds learn which foods to eat by copying the adult birds.

Did you spot the ten differences?

1 The female grizzly bear has a fish.

2 A gray wolf cub is now black.

3 A white-tailed deer has antlers.

4 The striped skunk's tail has moved.

5 The beavers are pushing a branch.

6 A coyote pup is present.

7 The puma cub's tail can be seen.

8 The woodpecker chick's beak is open.

9 One blue jay's egg is now a chick.

10 A raccoon has caught a crayfish.

6

Getting Around

Animals move around in many different ways. Look at this scene in Northern Europe. Can you match the footprints with the six animals in the small pictures? Look again. Can you see some other animals moving?

Many animals move around and some travel long distances every day. Animals can move in many different ways.

Most furry mammals have four legs (or two legs and two arms), but even these are used in different ways. Many mammals, such as the fallow deer, walk or run on their four legs. The deer's long, straight legs are built for running and galloping fast.

Rabbits can walk a little, but they mostly hop. They put their two front paws forward. Then they quickly bring the back ones up behind. Their long back legs and feet allow rabbits to make quite long leaps.

Squirrels run and leap. They use their sharp claws to cling to the bark as they run up and down trees.

27

Nature Trails

Squirrels can jump big distances between trees, too. They use their long tail as a balance when they scamper over thin branches. Red squirrels are found throughout Northern Europe and Asia. In most of southern England the Eastern gray squirrel has taken their place. The gray squirrel was introduced from North America.

Other mammals use their feet in different ways. Water voles walk on land. In the water, they use their feet to paddle themselves along. The mole burrows underground. Its front legs are short and strong. They have large claws that are excellent tools for digging.

Like many birds, the pheasant feeds on the ground. It spends most of its time walking on its two legs. Each foot is carefully placed in front of the other. Pheasants can fly, but only over short distances. The swallow is the complete opposite. It spends most of its life in the air. The swallow catches flying insects high up in the sky.

Snakes wriggle across the ground. They throw their bodies into a series of zigzag-shaped curves. Each curve acts like a foot and helps push the snake along.

Snails have only one foot. It forms the whole of the underside of their body. As the snail moves, the underside of the foot makes tiny folds. These push the snail along.

Spiders have eight legs. They can walk and run. They also swing for great distances, hanging by a thread of silk called gossamer.

Fingers for flying

Bats are small furry mammals. They fly like a bird, but their wings are made of skin. Each wing is stretched between the bat's tail, foot, arm, and fingertips.

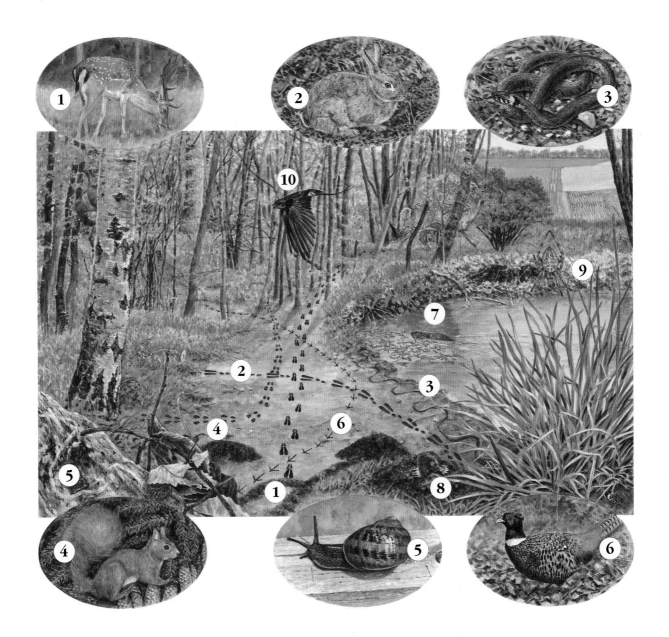

Who made the footprints?

1 Fallow deer and footprints.

2 Rabbit and paw prints.

3 Grass snake and trail.

4 Red squirrel and footprints.

5 Garden snail and slime trail.

6 Pheasant and footprints.

Did you find the other animals in the main picture?

7 Water vole swimming.

8 Mole digging a burrow.

9 Garden spider swinging.

10 Swallow flying.

Hunters and the Hunted

The plains of East Africa are home to many animals. Many are peaceful grazers, feeding on plants. Others eat meat. They hunt other animals. Look at this picture. A young gazelle (A) is separated from the herd. Can you help it find the one clear, safe path back to the herd (B)?

The grasslands of Africa are home to herds of grazing animals. Zebras, gazelles, and giraffes wander these plains. Many birds live here, too, including the ostrich. These animals must be constantly watching for predators who may attack them. Young, old, and sick animals are most at risk. Healthy adults can often outrun or chase away their attackers. Young animals sometimes get separated from the herd. They are very lucky if they survive to return to their parents.

There are many **species**, or kinds, of gazelles living in Africa. Grant's gazelle live in small herds of up to 30 animals. Many herds live in the same area grazing on the grass and shrubs. These herds provide food for many **predators**.

Tropical grasslands of Africa

The tropical grassland of Africa is called the savanna. Here it is hot all year. Winter is the wet season. Lush grasses grow after the rains have fallen. Many animals come to the savannas to graze on the fresh, green plants. The summer is very hot and no rain falls. It is the dry season. The grass becomes parched and dry. Many animals die from lack of water and food.

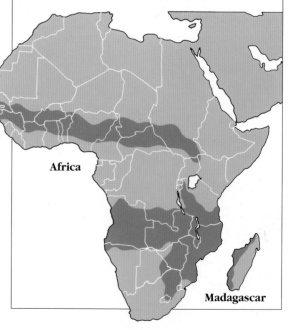

Africa

Madagascar

On the Run

A pride of lions rests beneath a tree. The lionesses do most of the hunting. They creep up on their **prey** before making a last running attack. The lioness kills its prey by biting the back of its neck. Males feed first, then the rest of the pride.

African hunting dogs hunt in a well-organized pack. They chase a large animal, attacking it many times. Their prey becomes weak and tired. It finally falls to the ground and is killed by these wild dogs.

The cheetah stalks its prey, which are mostly gazelles. When close enough, the cheetah starts to chase its prey. The fastest land animal, it can run at up to 70 miles (112 km) an hour. This uses up a lot of energy and the cheetah quickly

In for the kill

Lions, cheetahs, and other large predators not only catch grazing animals, but they also kill each other. Lions will kill the cubs of other lions and cheetah cubs. The mother cheetah always hides her cubs when she is away. Hyenas also kill hunting dog pups and cheetah cubs. No animal is safe on the plains.

Cheetah and cubs

Lionesses and cubs

becomes tired. The chase often takes less than a minute. If its prey starts to get away, the cheetah gives up. It looks for another kill.

Leopards hunt at night. They catch small animals and drag their kill up into a tree. This stops hyenas and other animals from stealing it. The leopard sleeps most of the day, often draped over a branch in its favorite tree.

Carrion feeders, such as hyenas and vultures, eat dead animals. They soon remove all that remains of any animal that is killed. Hyenas eat everything, including the skin, bones, and hair. Nothing is wasted. Hyenas are also very fierce. They will chase a cheetah or lion from its kill. Packs of hyenas also hunt. They will attack zebras and other large grazers.

Vultures fly high overhead. When they see a carcass or other vultures gathering, they swoop down to join the feast. The vulture uses its powerful hooked bill to cut the flesh of the dead animal.

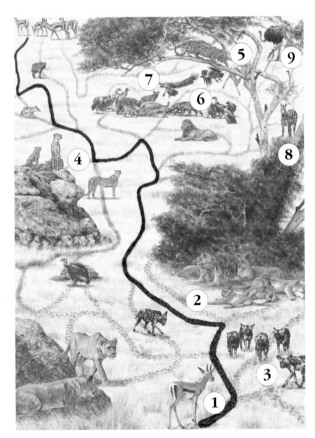

Animals of the savanna

1   Grant's gazelle.
2   Lions with cubs.
3   Hunting dogs.
4   Cheetah and cubs.
5   Leopard with prey.
6   Spotted hyena.
7   Vulture.
8   Zebra.
9   Ostrich.

Animal Architects

Most animals make themselves some sort of nest or home. A few are outstanding architects. Look at the picture opposite. Can you match each of the six animals with its amazing home?

Animals build a home to provide a safe place to sleep and rear their young. The home may have special areas for storing food or rearing young. In the case of a garden spider's web, the home itself may be used to trap food.

Male weaver birds build very complex nests. The nest is woven from grass and soft twigs. A male makes many nests, one for each female in his territory. Different weaver birds build different kinds of nests. The masked weaver in East Africa finishes his nest with a short entrance on the side. Baya weaver birds in India make long entrance tubes that point downward. This stops snakes from entering the nests to steal the bird's eggs.

Beavers build such large homes that they divert rivers and change the landscape. They cut down trees and pull them into the water to build a dam across a stream. The beavers build a lodge in the middle of the pond that forms behind the dam. The lodge looks like a pile of sticks.

Weaver bird nests

Weaver birds start to build their nests by making a loop or ring of grass. This is tied and woven onto the tip of a branch. More grass is woven around this until a ball-shaped nest is made. Some birds, like the sociable weavers, build a communal nest. Each pair of birds has its own entrance and nest.

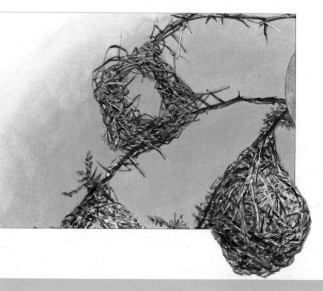

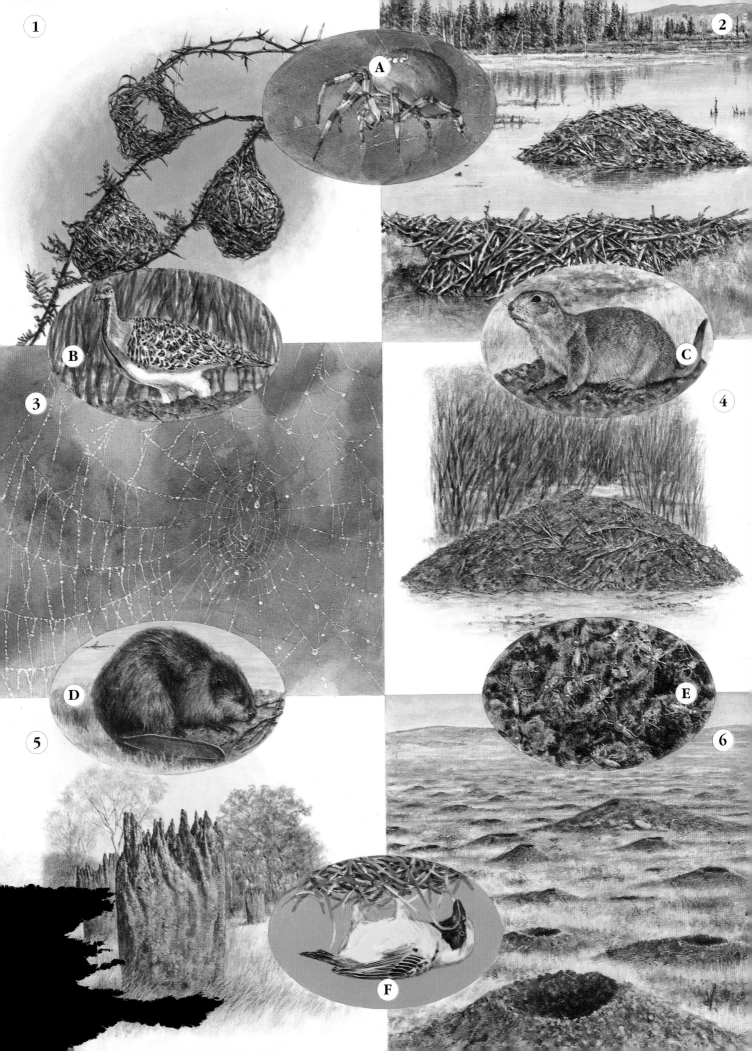

Home, Sweet Home

Inside the beaver's lodge is a safe home. An underwater entrance leads to a warm, dry den. Here the beavers spend the winter and raise their young in safety.

Orb-web spiders, such as the garden spider, spin beautiful, lacy webs. These are nets to catch flying insects. The webs are stretched between twigs in a bush or against a fence. The spider sits at the center of the web and waits for prey. When an insect gets caught, the spider runs across to kill it.

Mallee fowl are large birds like turkeys that live in Australia. In winter, the male digs a pit and fills it with pieces of plants. He covers it with sand. As the plant material rots, the nest gets hot. The male

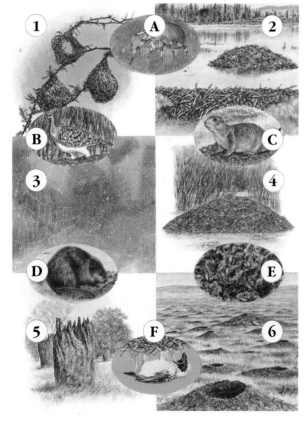

Did you match the animals with their homes?

1: **F** Masked weaver bird and nest.
2: **D** Beaver and lodge.
3: **A** Garden spider and web.
4: **B** Mallee fowl and nest.
5: **E** Compass termite and mound.
6: **C** Prairie dog and underground home.

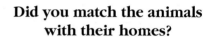
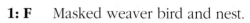

checks the temperature. If the nest is too hot, he opens it up. If it is too cool, he piles on more sand. The female lays her eggs in the mound. The chicks hatch after about seven weeks and scramble out. They soon start to feed themselves and can fly within a day.

Termites live in a colony and build huge nests called termite mounds. Compass termites from Australia build tall, narrow mounds. The thin edge of the mound always points in a north–south direction.

In this way, the narrow side of the mound points towards the midday sun. This ensures that the nest does not become too hot.

Prairie dogs live in the grasslands of North America. They tunnel out huge underground "towns." Each main tunnel has an opening at either end. One opens on the flat land of the prairies. The other is marked by a mound up to a foot high. Air is drawn out of the upper entrance and flows in to the lower entrance. This airflow keeps the nest fresh.

Termite mounds

Termites are small antlike insects that live in a large colony. Each colony has a queen termite that produces millions of eggs. These eggs hatch into worker termites. Some remain workers all their lives, while others become nurses and look after the young. Soldier termites have large jaws and protect the colony. At certain times of the year, winged males and females fly off to start a new colony. Termite mounds are massive structures. Different species build different shapes. Mounds are heated by rotting fragments of plant material. Fresh air is circulated throughout the colony by special air passages. The termites control the airflow by closing or opening passages. Termite

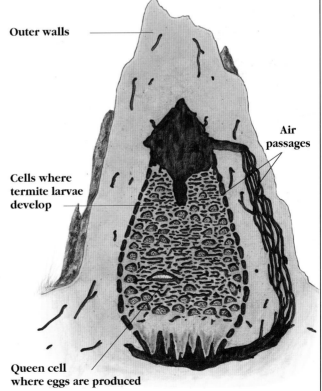

Outer walls

Air passages

Cells where termite larvae develop

Queen cell where eggs are produced

37

9

Look at Me!

When seeking a mate, many birds perform courtship displays. Male bowerbirds of New Guinea build very complex homes to attract the females. The birds of paradise have bright colored plumage. Look at these picture of a forest scene in New Guinea. Can you spot the ten differences between them?

Most animals need to find a mate before they can have young. Male animals use courtship displays to attract a mate. The males often compete, and the biggest show-off wins the female. Male animals have many ways of attracting mates.

In New Guinea and Australia, the male bowerbird is dull colored. He cannot use bright feathers to attract a mate. Instead, he builds a special nest called a bower. Each species of male bowerbird builds a different type of bower. He decorates the bower with flowers and berries. Some bowers are simple wide lanes of grass, others are more complex. The best bower attracts the female.

Dressing Up

Australia and New Guinea

The plants and animals of Australia and New Guinea are very similar. Millions of years ago Australia and New Guinea split away from the main land mass. This main land mass later became the continents of the rest of the world. Most of the mammals that lived in Australia at that time were marsupials. A few were even more primitive mammals that laid eggs. These mammals continued to develop into the Australian creatures that we know today. In the rest of the world marsupials died out. They were replaced by the more advanced placental mammals such as cats and dogs.

The cuscus is a marsupial and carries its young in a pouch.

The long-beaked echidna lays eggs.

In New Guinea, MacGregor's bowerbird builds a decorated pole of twigs stuck into the stem of a small tree. A low wall of moss surrounds the area around the pole. The striped gardener bowerbird builds a more complex structure. A little hut is covered with a grass roof. In front, a lawn of moss is protected by a fence. When a female appears, the male displays to her in the bower.

Birds of paradise are brightly colored. The male king bird of paradise and bluebird of paradise have similar displays. They hang upside down from a branch. The male fans out his splendid feathers. He shakes the feathers, making a strange buzzing sound. He waves his long tail plumes to attract a female. The best display will win the mate.

Many other rare animals live in these forests of New Guinea. The long-beaked echidna is a primitive mammal that lays eggs. It feeds on termites and ants. The cuscus and tree kangaroos are marsupials, related to the koalas of Australia.

Did you spot the ten differences?

1   The male striped gardener bowerbird's fence is now complete.

2   Another flower is in the bower.

3   The male gardener bowerbird has a fruit in his beak.

4   The eyestripe of the king bird of paradise is present.

5   The male MacGregor's bowerbird's crest is flattened.

6   The female MacGregor's bowerbird is present.

7   The tree kangaroo is now eating leaves.

8   The cuscus's tail is coiled around a branch.

9   The long-beaked echidna has its tongue out.

10 The male bluebird of paradise has one tail feather missing.

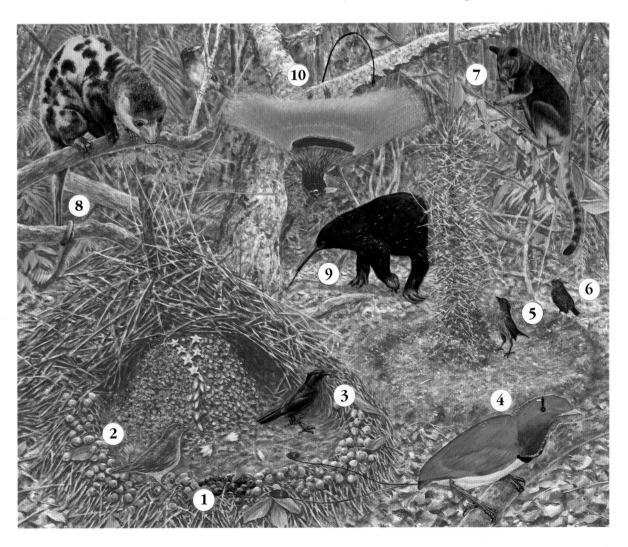

Finding the Way

Each year many birds make long journeys between their winter and summer homes. Look at this map. Can you find the summer nesting places of the six birds shown in the small pictures? Can you find the path these birds take to their winter feeding grounds?

Many mammals, birds, and fish make long trips called migrations. They migrate away from places where the weather is bad or food is scarce. Some birds fly a long way when they migrate. Modern satellite tracking and putting a band on a bird's leg can be used to track birds. This way scientists find out where birds go.

In North America, Europe, and Northern Asia, many kinds of birds spend the summer feeding and breeding in the North. In autumn, they fly south to spend the winter in southern Africa or South America where it is then summer. In this way the birds avoid the cold and have two seasons of summer food.

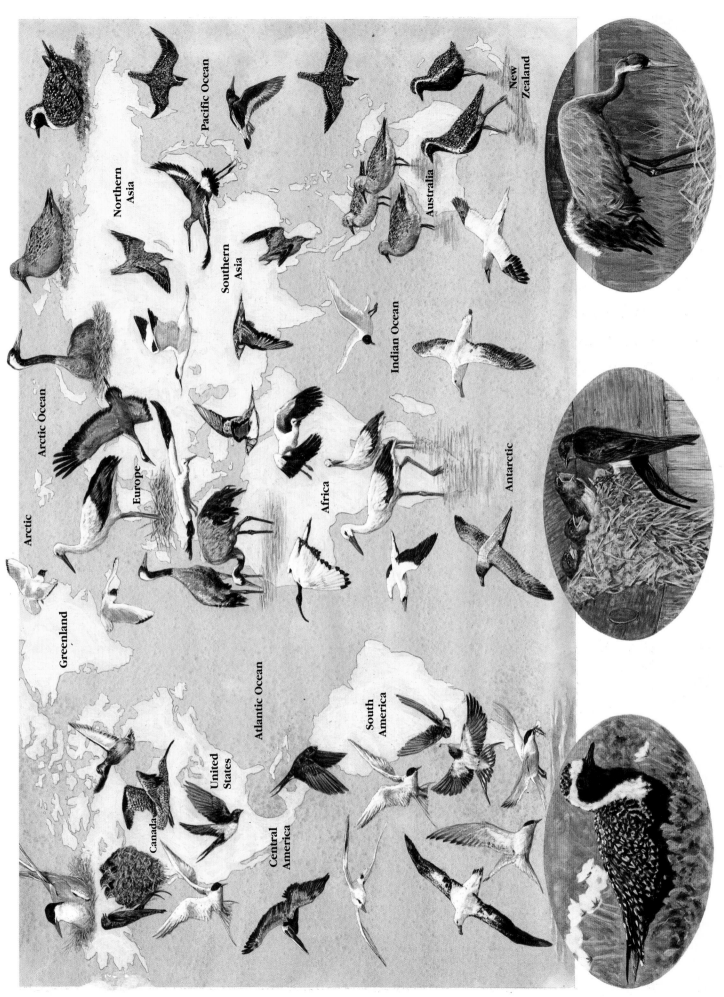

Northern Asia

Pacific Ocean

New Zealand

Southern Asia

Australia

Indian Ocean

Arctic

Arctic Ocean

Europe

Africa

Antarctic

Greenland

Atlantic Ocean

South America

United States

Canada

Central America

43

New Pastures

Migrating birds

1   Knots fly from the Arctic to Australia.

2   Arctic terns fly from the Arctic to the Antarctic.

3   White storks fly from northern Europe to Africa.

4   Lesser golden plovers fly from the Arctic to Australia.

5   Swallows fly from the Arctic to South America.

6   Cranes fly from Europe to North Africa.

Migration by land and sea

Many other types of animals migrate. Whales swim from the Antarctic to northern oceans. Salmon and eels return to the rivers of Northern Europe and North America. On land, caribou migrate to the Arctic tundra and back. In Africa, wildebeest follow the rains in search of fresh grass. Fragile monarch butterflies migrate for hundreds of miles. They cross the land and sea to reach their breeding grounds or winter roosts, the place where they settle.

Monarch butterfly

Wildebeest

they fly south to spend the winter on the **estuaries** of Europe and North America. The European white stork uses warm air currents to help it fly from Europe to southern Africa. Cranes, too, migrate from the cold in eastern Europe. They spend the winter feeding in northern Africa.

Arctic terns make some of the longest journeys. They fly thousands of miles from the Arctic to the Antarctic each year. The lesser golden plover and the knot also make long journeys. They nest in the Far North. Then, when the bitterly cold winter threatens, they leave. They fly south to Australia to their feeding grounds.

The swallow breeds in northern Europe and North America. In autumn, the bird flies south to Africa or South America to avoid the northern winter. This ensures that the swallow always has enough insects to eat.

In summer, many ducks and shore birds breed in the Far North on the Arctic tundra. In autumn,

No one is quite sure how these birds find their way. Some birds fly alone. Others follow their parents or fly in a flock. Scientists believe that migrant animals use the sun and the stars and Earth's magnetic field to guide them. Birds may also follow distant sounds and smells carried on the wind. Many birds and other animals return to exactly the same nesting sites each year. The young birds will also return to the place where they were born.

Glossary

Burrow A tunnel that many kinds of animals dig in the ground. Some animals live in their burrows. Others just use them to find food, sleep in, or as a nest for their young.

Colony A group of living things of the same kind that live together.

Dominant In nature, an animal that has a high position or rank in its group – the "boss." Dominant animals usually get the best food, shelter, and mates compared to the younger or "lesser" members.

Den A hole in a burrow, a cave, or a similar place where an animal rests and sleeps. Sometimes animals raise their young in a den.

Estuary The mouth of a river where the fresh water mixes with sea water.

Extinct Describes a kind of living thing that has completely died out.

Herd A large number of grazing animals of the same kind that feed and travel around together.

Larva (plural **larvae**) The young of certain animals, such as frogs, crustaceans, some insects, and some fish. A larva hatches from the egg and often looks quite different from its parents.

Life cycle The stages that a living thing goes through during its life. In an insect, it begins with the egg. In some insects the egg hatches into a larva. The larva changes into a pupa, or chrysalis. The pupa splits, and the adult insect crawls free.

Marsupial One of a group of mammals whose young are born at a very early stage. Most marsupials carry their young in a pouch.

Moor An area of high land that is covered by coarse grass, heather, and coarse ferns.

Nest A special place made and lived in by an animal. Some animals lay their eggs or bring up their young in a nest.

Nymph The young form of some types of insects, such as dragonflies.

Predator An animal that kills and eats other animals.

Prey An animal that is killed and eaten by another animal.

Pupa (plural **pupae**) The stage in the life cycle of an insect that follows the larva.

Species A group of living things that look similar. They can mate and produce young.

Territory An area of land or water in which an animal, or group of animals, lives.

Tundra Regions of the world where it is too cold for trees to grow.

Index

A Templar Book

Devised and produced by The Templar Company plc
Pippbrook Mill, London Road, Dorking, Surrey RH4 1JE, G   Britain
© Copyright 1996 by The Templar Company